Group Mem

Second Guessing God

A 7-week Bible Study by

BRIAN JONES

Standard®
PUBLISHING
Bringing The Word to Life

Cincinnati, Ohio

Second Guessing God, ISBN 0-7847-1841-5, text © Brian Jones

Printed in the United States of America.

Project editor: Michael Mack
Cover design: by Scott Ryan, based on design by The DesignWorks™ Group
Interior design: Robert Korth

ISBN 0-7847-1958-6

13 12 11 10 09 08 07 9 8 7 6 5 4 3 2 1

CONTENTS

How to Use This Guide

This guide is designed for group use with the companion book, *Second Guessing God.* It will help your group discuss the ideas from *Second Guessing God* and apply them in your lives. This happens best in groups that are growing together in real friendships, real faith, and even real fun!

True to the Bible

The aim is not to study a book, however. It is to study God's Word, using *Second Guessing God* as a launching pad. We have designed this guide, like all the Standard Publishing products you've come to trust, to be true to the Bible.

True to Life

We designed this guide also to be true to life—life in the real world of spouses, kids, jobs, bills, and everyday circumstances. We want this guide to help your faith intersect with real life, so you will live the life that Jesus promised: life to the full!

A number of features make this guide distinctive:

- *It is designed for busy people.* You will not need to spend hours preparing for meetings, whether you are the leader or another member of the group. At the same time, reading the companion book, *Second Guessing God,* is highly recommended to help you get the most out of this study.
- *It is designed for people at various maturity levels.* You do not need to be a Bible scholar to facilitate or participate in these studies. The companion book will provide the "teaching" each week. Your job is to discuss and apply the truths from God's Word to your lives.

- *It is designed to develop community.* Your group—whether you are a Sunday school class, Bible study, or small group—will grow closer to one another as you share your stories, study the Word, and serve together. The optimal number of participants in a group is usually about three to ten, depending on a variety of circumstances. But larger groups can still be very effective. We suggest you subgroup if your group is larger than twelve. You may want to break into several groups of three to six during the Study and Apply sections, for instance, for deeper discussion and more authentic application.
- *It is designed to help you grow spiritually.* Real, lasting life change is the primary goal. The Holy Spirit will transform you as you allow Him to work through God's Word and other group members to encourage, support, admonish, and pray for one another. Your group will employ Colossians 3:16: "Let the word of Christ dwell in you richly as you teach and admonish one another with all wisdom."

For the Leader
You are in a vital position to help people grow in their relationships with God. The best leadership comes out of the overflow of a godly leader's heart. The "Leader Preparation" section and other leader helps are included to feed your heart first—to equip and encourage you before you lead your group. God has called you to shepherd this small group of people that He has entrusted to your care. We want to provide whatever support and resources we can to help you carry out this vital ministry to which God has called you. See the article from SmallGroups.com in the Appendix to help you grow as a spiritual leader and shepherd.

How Each Session Is Organized

Leader Preparation: Use this section to prepare your heart and mind for the meeting. To maximize opportunities for spiritual growth in your group, take time to read and reflect. Also, use this time to pray for group members.

Bible Study Agenda: This is an inductive rather than deductive study. It is designed to help participants discover truth from God's Word through group interaction rather than just telling them what it says. It is also designed to help participants observe, contemplate, wrestle with, and take action on Scripture. Use the questions to facilitate lively interaction among group members. This will lead people to "aha" moments—when they "get it." Ask follow-up questions to keep a good discussion moving. Keep the group on track with strong yet gentle encouragement and guidance.

- *Connect:* Before the meeting, ask a group member to read the excerpt from *Second Guessing God.* This will help focus participants' minds on the topic. Utilize the Connect questions to help group members share about what they know best—themselves—and get them actively involved in the discussion. The main question here is, "What is your story?"
- *Study:* These discussion questions are arranged to help members first observe and examine the Bible text, then understand and discern what the Scripture means and how they relate to it personally. The question here is, "What is God saying to you in this passage?"
- *Apply:* This is the most important meeting element. Make sure you move the group toward this part of the process. Here they will relate God's Word to their own everyday lives and decide what they will do with it. The question here is, "How will I respond?"

Before the Next Meeting: Encourage group members to read the next chapter(s) in *Second Guessing God* for the upcoming meeting. They may also look up Scripture passages if they like, but they do not need to do any "homework" other than what's listed here.

Leaders Between-Meeting Shepherding Ideas: A healthy, life-changing small group is more than just a once-a-week meeting. This section will help you as a leader to shepherd group members between meetings. Set an example by staying in contact with participants between meetings though phone calls, visits, e-mail, and personal letters or cards. The best groups are like close families that care for one another 24-7.

SESSION ONE

Upstream

You will lead me by the right road, though I may know nothing about it. Therefore I will trust you always though I may seem to be lost and in the shadow of death. I will not fear, for you are ever with me, and you will never leave me to face my perils alone.[1]

—*Thomas Merton*

Leader Preparation

- ❏ Have you ever asked "Where's God?" When? Why? How did you work through this spiritual dilemma? Be prepared to transparently share your experience with your group.
- ❏ Read *Second Guessing God* chapters 1–2 and Joshua 3:1-17.
- ❏ Read this lesson beforehand, jotting down your observations and questions as they arise.

CONNECT

Where's God? It's a question that graces the headlines of major world newspapers. It comes up on talk shows. Kids wonder about it. Universities create courses to discuss it. It's the question everyone asks when the storms of life hit. Perhaps the most interesting thing about this question, however, is that people ask it regardless of where they are in their spiritual walk.

Spiritual skeptics ask this question. Elton John recorded a song that asks, "If there's a God in heaven, what's he waiting for?"[2] In the past few years, I've listened to the difficult stories of hundreds of spiritual skeptics. Based on what I've heard, I believe the song asks a fair question. When I first became a pastor, I thought that those who opposed the idea of God were just being stubborn. Now I humbly tell people that I've never met an atheist who didn't have a good reason for being one.

Spiritual inquirers ask the question too. Every year I teach a sermon series called "Questions I Want to Ask God." To prepare, I give everyone an index card and ask them to tell me, "If you could ask God only one question and you knew he would give you an answer, what would you ask?" After the cards are collected, I pick four of the questions and try to answer them over the next four weeks. People tell me they love the series because I'm answering their questions. Yet one of the biggest challenges I have doing this year after year is keeping the material fresh. It's no exaggeration to say that almost half the cards, every year, ask the same question in some form: *where's God?*

1. If *you* could ask God only one question and you knew he would give you an answer, what would *you* ask?

Many assume that after you've followed Jesus for a long time, you're somehow exempt from ever thinking dark thoughts about God. Unfortunately, you aren't. Even seasoned believers ask the question. When C. S. Lewis lost his wife, Joy, to cancer, he wrote in his journal:

> Meanwhile, where is God? This is one of the most disquieting symptoms. When you are happy, so happy that you have no sense of needing Him, so happy that you are tempted to feel His claims upon you as an interruption, if you remember yourself and turn to Him with gratitude and praise, you will be—or so it feels—welcomed with open arms. But go to Him when your need is desperate, when all other help is vain, and what do you find? A door slammed in your face, and a sound of bolting and double bolting on the inside. After that, silence. You may as well turn away. The longer you wait, the more emphatic the silence will become.[3]

The Big Picture

The Bible tells us that for over four hundred years God's people were slaves in Egypt, until God raised up Moses to lead them out of bondage. After their miraculous escape, God did not instruct the people to build a city immediately outside the borders of Egypt. Instead, he told them to follow as he led them to the land he had promised centuries ago to their forefather Abraham, a place of abundance, flowing with milk and honey.

Because of their disobedience, however, a journey that should have taken a month or so eventually took forty years. Now those who were children when they escaped Egypt stood with *their* children and viewed the promised land with their own eyes. —*Second Guessing God,* p. 33

The Inside Story

On maps the Jordan River valley looks like a roller coaster. One scholar calls it "the earth's deepest valley."[4] The Jordan River begins at the Sea of Galilee and travels just over sixty miles south, where it empties into the Dead Sea, the lowest place on the planet, thirteen hundred feet below sea level. Most of the year it is a tranquil, meandering river, but during harvest season the rainwater converges in the valley basin, and it becomes a swollen torrent.

—*Second Guessing God*, p. 34

2. Has there ever been a time in your life when you felt like God "slammed a door" in your face and double bolted it on the inside?

STUDY

Read Joshua 3:1-17.

3. What do you think the Israelites talked about as they sat by the campfire the night before crossing over into the promised land?

4. The ark of the covenant was a gold-encrusted box that held the tablets inscribed with the Ten Commandments. What might be the significance of the priests carrying the ark ahead of the people?

5. Verse 15 adds one tiny little detail to the story: "Now the Jordan is at flood stage all during harvest." What do you think would have happened if the Israelites tried to cross the Jordan without God's supernatural intervention?

6. Read verse 16 again. Imagine you are one of the Israelites. What are you thinking when you see the river has stopped flowing?

The Main Idea

Did you catch that? *As soon as the priests' feet touched the water,* God caused the water to stop flowing. In fact, the Bible later tells us that the water stopped completely, the riverbed dried up, and God's people were able to cross over on dry ground. Where did God stop the flow of water? Did it stop right where the people were standing? Did the Israelites see God at work with their own eyes? No. The water "piled up in a heap a great distance away, at a town called Adam" (v. 16).

Scholars estimate the town of Adam was roughly nineteen miles upstream from where the Israelites stood, far beyond where they could see. It was a miracle, but it was a miracle the people didn't witness with their own eyes. God performed the miracle upstream, out of their sight.

I believe the same situation occurs in our lives today. Here's the powerful truth the children of Israel learned that day: *God is always at work upstream in our lives.*

Where's God? Whenever we face a problem in our lives—sickness, job loss, depression, tragedy, or discouragement—God is at work *upstream* in those situations, beyond our line of sight. The only thing the Israelites could see was the problem right in front of them. They could have concluded that since that raging river was there, God wasn't actively involved in their situation, but they would have been wrong. He was there; they just couldn't see him at work.

—*Second Guessing God,* p. 35

APPLY

7. Like the Israelites, have you ever faced what appeared to be an impossible situation but realized later that God was working upstream all along?

8. The book mentions three important things to do when trying to "see" God at work upstream in our problems. Share with the group which one you are struggling to allow to happen and why:

- "I need to learn to trust what I can't see."
- "I need to learn to let go of what I can't control."
- "I need to see my pain within the bigger picture of God's plan."

Together, read this final challenge from the book:

At the church I serve, I've taught about God working upstream many times, and over the years it has become a mantra among the people in the congregation. I hear it repeated all the time.

Something happens to someone—a bad report from the doctor, a child going through hard times, relationship difficulties—and I'll overhear someone else say, "Let me pray for you. God is working upstream in your life right now. Let's pray that he gives you the strength to hold on until you find out what he's doing."

Leader Follow-up
Encourage group members to pass their Participant's Guide around the group and have their fellow group members place their names and e-mail addresses (or phone numbers) inside. As needs arise between meetings, encourage group members to e-mail one another their prayer requests.

9. As you begin this study together, make praying for one another a natural part of your group's spiritual DNA. Close your time together by praying for the person on your right. Pray for whatever prayer concerns they share, especially that God will help them with their answer to question eight.

Before the next meeting:

- Read chapters 1–3 and 6 in *Second Guessing God.*
- Underline anything that you learn for the first time or are inspired by or have a question about.

NOTES

[1]Thomas Merton, *Thoughts in Solitude* (New York: Farrar, Strauss and Giroux, 1958), 79.

[2]Elton John, Davey Johnstone, and Bernie Taupin, "If There's a God in Heaven (What's He Waiting For?)," *Blue Moves* (MCA, 1976).

[3]C. S. Lewis, *A Grief Observed* (New York: HarperCollins, 1994), 21–22.

[4]E. G. Kraeling, quoted in Marten H. Woudstra, *The Book of Joshua: The New International Commentary on the Old Testament* (Grand Rapids: Eerdmans, 1981), 58.

SESSION TWO

Power

Leader Preparation

- ❑ When was the last time you prayed for God to work a miracle in your life? Did he grant your request? Is your experience normal? Why? Why not?
- ❑ Read *Second Guessing God* chapters 3 and 6 and 2 Corinthians 4:7-11.
- ❑ Read this lesson beforehand, jotting down your observations and questions as they arise.

To be a witness does not consist in engaging propaganda, nor even in stirring people up, but in being a living mystery. It means to live in such a way that one's life would not make sense if God did not exist.[1]

—*Cardinal Emmanuel Suhard*

CONNECT

What does every miracle in the Bible have in common? Every miracle in the Bible is preceded by a problem. Problems and miracles go hand in hand. You can't seem to go too far with one without finding the other. From God's vantage point, difficulty is the breeding ground for the miraculous. However, the Bible seems to show us that there are *two* different kinds of miracles, not just one.

Instantaneous miracles. The first kind of miracle is where God supernaturally removes or resolves a problem, like when someone is physically ill and God removes the sickness. I call these "instantaneous miracles" because they happen in a moment's notice. The apostle Paul performed instantaneous miracles. "God did extraordinary miracles through Paul" (Acts 19:11). These miracles were immediate. Presto, chango–it's done. Cancer's gone. Sight's restored.

1. Share a time with the group when you or someone you know experienced an instantaneous miracle.

Perseverance miracles. The second kind of miracle is the kind where God chooses not to supernaturally remove or resolve a problem. Instead, God gives his ongoing, miraculous strength to us to enable us to persevere through the problem. This kind of miracle happened routinely in the Bible, and it still happens as frequently today. I call these "perseverance miracles" because the "miracle" does not occur instantly. James 1:3 tells us that "the testing of [our] faith develops perseverance." The Greek word for perseverance is *hypoméno.* It's formed by the combination of two Greek words: *hypo,* under, and *meno,* to remain. To persevere means to stand up under a heavy trial, the way a bodybuilder lifts three hundred pounds over his head and stands up under it—arms shaking, knees ready to buckle, shoulders splitting with pain—without dropping the weights.

There were times in the Bible when God chose not to instantaneously heal people. Paul ends one of his letters by saying, "I left Trophimus sick in Miletus" (2 Timothy 4:20). Sick? Trophimus was Paul's coworker. Doesn't the Bible say God performed "extraordinary miracles" through Paul? Surely God could have healed Trophimus, but he didn't. Instead, God chose to give Trophimus the strength to persevere through his sickness.

2. Has there ever been a time when you've felt like Trophimus? God had the power to heal you or change your circumstances and chose not to do so? Why do you think he did that?

The Big Picture

"Jars of clay" is a powerful analogy. At the time Paul wrote this passage, clay pottery, dishes, and cookware were common. Clayware was common because it was so inexpensive to make—clay from the ground and fire to harden it were all that was needed. "Jars of clay" were also very brittle. Our minds and bodies are a lot like those jars of clay. We're frail. We break. We crack and fall to pieces. Clay pots don't hold up real well under extramarital affairs, depression, and bankruptcy. When we manage to keep our lives intact when they should be scattered across the floor in a million pieces, we—and others—realize that something supernatural is holding us together.

—*Second Guessing God*, pp. 54, 55

STUDY

Read 2 Corinthians 4:7-11.

3. What do you think Paul is referring to when he uses the word *treasure*?

4. How would housing this treasure in jars of clay show that this all-surpassing power is from God and not from us?

5. Brainstorm other modern day metaphors that could replace "jars of clay" in this passage. Why did you pick those?

6. Paul uses four phrases to describe what his life was like: hard-pressed, perplexed, persecuted, and struck down. Do you think every Christian, at some point in his or her spiritual walk, will experience one or all of these, or was Paul's experience unusual? What has been your experience so far?

7. What do you think Paul was trying to say when he wrote, "We always carry around in our body the death of Jesus"?

The Inside Story

God does his best work over long periods of time. That is important to remember. The Bible is a compilation of sixty-six different books written over two thousand years. It just *seems as if* God performed miracles in people's lives all the time because the Bible condenses thousands of years of history into one book. If we don't keep this in mind, we can get a distorted impression of what it was like to live back then. God didn't deliver miracles every day like the morning newspaper. Most followers of God went their whole lives without witnessing one supernatural intervention on the part of heaven. With some exceptions, the majority of people who lived in biblical times experienced life just as we experience it today.

—*Second Guessing God*, pp. 51, 52

The Main Idea

One of the reasons I think God performs more perseverance miracles than instantaneous miracles is because their impact is longer. They stretch. Perseverance miracles aren't flash-in-the-pan. When someone perseveres in the midst of unspeakable hardship, her presence and joy leaves no one untouched. It seeps into boardrooms and kitchens, bowling alleys and nursing stations, front porches and bus stops. Being a living miracle has a much more lasting effect over time on everyone you come in contact with than do miracles that come and go like the wind. That's why, I think, if you give God the choice between instantly healing someone or giving him miraculous strength to live with joy, it's clear which one God will choose and why. When you look at it this way, it's a wonder God performs any instantaneous miracles at all.

—*Second Guessing God*, pp. 60, 61

APPLY

8. Have you ever experienced a perseverance miracle? What kind of impact did it have on you? What impact did it have on those around you?

9. Think back to all the times in your life when you prayed for an instantaneous miracle. How would your life be different if God had granted every single one of those requests? Would your life be better? worse? about the same?

10. What do you think someone in the middle of a perseverance miracle needs to hear?

Together, read this final challenge from the book:

> When we realize that God wants us to experience a perseverance miracle rather than an instantaneous miracle, it is easy to become bitter, withdrawn, and negative. During those dark times it helps to have someone in your life who has walked in your shoes before. Every Trophimus needs a Paul.

11. End your time together by praying for one another in the group, especially those in the midst of a perseverance miracle. Pick a "Paul" to say the final prayer.

Leader Follow-up
Encourage group members to keep track of the kinds of prayers they pray this week. Do they find themselves asking for more instantaneous miracles or perseverance miracles?

Before the next meeting:

- Read chapters 4 and 7 in *Second Guessing God.*
- Underline anything that you learn for the first time or are inspired by or have a question about.

NOTES

[1]Cardinal Emmanuel Suhard, quoted in Madeleine L'Engle, *Walking on Water: Reflections on Faith and Art* (Colorado Springs: Waterbrook Press, 2004), 26.

SESSION THREE

Compassion

The most beautiful people we have known are those who have known defeat, known suffering, known struggle, known loss, and have found their way out of the depths. These persons have an appreciation, a sensitivity and an understanding of life that fills them with compassion, gentleness, and a deep loving concern. Beautiful people do not just happen.[1]

—Elisabeth Kubler-Ross

Leader Preparation

- ❏ Do you have any "beautiful people" in your life? Take a moment and reflect on what you learned from their examples.
- ❏ Read *Second Guessing God* chapters 4 and 7 and Philippians 1:1-8.
- ❏ Read this lesson beforehand, jotting down your observations and questions as they arise.

CONNECT

1. If you saw a complete stranger crying outside a department store, which animal would best depict how you would respond to that person? Be honest!

- ❏ Owl—"I'd keep an eye on him but from a safe distance."
- ❏ Cat—"I'd reach out to him but on my own terms."
- ❏ Golden Retriever—"I'd run up to him and hug him."
- ❏ Porcupine—"I'd get a little closer but not too close."
- ❏ Lion—"I'd growl and wonder what he was complaining about."

Thornton Wilder's short play, "The Angel That Troubled the Waters," is based on a tradition described in the Bible in John 5. In the city of Jerusalem was a pool of water known as the Pool of Bethesda. According to the tradition, from time to time an angel came down to stir up the water, and the first person into the pool after each such disturbance would be cured of whatever disease he or she had. Naturally, then, people who were blind, lame, and paralyzed stayed near the pool day and night.

In Wilder's play a group of invalids sit at the water's edge as a physician walks into their midst and waits for an angel to stir the water. The invalids surrounding the pool scream at him to leave, but the physician explains that he struggles with severe depression and needs to be healed as much as any blind or lame person there that day. As they are talking, an angel suddenly appears. The doctor, in good physical health, lunges for the water. The angel, however, refuses to touch the water, preventing the physician from being healed. The physician sees his reluctance and pleads with him:

> Surely, surely, the angels are wise. Surely, O prince, you are not deceived by my apparent wholeness. Your eyes can see the nets in which my wings are caught. . . .

To which the angel replies:

> Without your wound where would your power be? It is your very remorse that makes your low voice tremble into the hearts of men. The very angels themselves cannot persuade the wretched and blundering children on earth as can one human being broken on the wheels of living. In love's service only the wounded soldiers can serve. Draw back.

Heartbroken, the physician steps back and watches the angel stir the water. Within seconds mangled bodies scrape and claw their way to the edge of the pool. A lucky invalid, the first to touch the water, screams for joy as he jumps up completely restored. As he runs around the pool showing everyone that he's been healed, the physician turns to walk away. Out of the corner of his eye, the newly healed man sees the physician leaving the pool. Moved by the doctor's misfortune, he runs up to him and says:

> Come with me . . . an hour only, to my home. My son is lost in dark thoughts. I—I do not understand him, and only you have ever lifted his mood. Only an hour . . . my daughter, since her child has died, sits in the shadow. She will not listen to us.[2]

And the play ends.

The Big Picture

Affection in Philippians 1:8 comes from the Greek word *splanchna*, which means "guts." Many times it was also translated "compassion." In the Bible *splanchna* is used literally to describe the inner parts of the chest cavity, such as the heart, lungs, and blood vessels, but it is also used figuratively to describe the overwhelming compassion someone feels towards another person in need. When I watch a sad movie, my jaw tightens, my chest constricts, I get a lump in my throat, my eyes water, my heart races. That's *splanchna*, an overwhelming feeling of compassion for another person.

—*Second Guessing God*, p. 76

2. Why do you think Wilder says that "in love's service only wounded soldiers can serve"?

3. Do you think only those who have experienced pain in their lives can be of service to others in pain? Why? Why not?

STUDY

Read Philippians 1:1-8.

4. Many point to Philippians 1:1-8 as some of the warmest words the apostle Paul wrote in all of his letters. Imagine that your group is the recipient of the letter to the Philippians. What specific comments does Paul make in that passage that would make your day?

5. In 1 Timothy 1:13 the apostle Paul tells us that before he became a Christian he was a "blasphemer and a persecutor and a violent man." The contrast between that description and the words of Philippians 1:1-8 is striking. Do you think Paul became an affectionate person because of his conversion to Christianity or as a result of the trials he experienced afterwards? Why?

6. Read 1 Corinthians 4:9-13. How would these specific trials have made Paul more compassionate? Is it possible to become more compassionate without suffering?

The Inside Story

Paul, however, went one step further and said that he had *Jesus'* affection and compassion for people, which led me to look up how the Bible uses *splanchna* in descriptions of the ministry of Jesus. I discovered that Jesus felt *compassion* for just about everyone he met:

"When Jesus landed and saw a large crowd, he had compassion *[splanchna]* on them, because they were like sheep without a shepherd" (Mark 6:34).

When Jesus saw a woman who had lost both her husband and only son, "his heart went out to her *[splanchna]* and he said, 'Don't cry'" (Luke 7:13).

In the story of the good Samaritan, Jesus said, "But a Samaritan, as he traveled, came where the man was; and when he saw him, he took pity *[splanchna]* on him" (Luke 10:33).

And in probably the most famous example, the story of the prodigal son, Jesus said, "But while he was still a long way off, his father saw him and was filled with compassion *[splanchna]* for him; he ran to his son, threw his arms around him and kissed him" (Luke 15:20).

After I finished reading these verses in the original Greek, I bowed my head and prayed, "Jesus, please give me the same affection for people that you have."

—*Second Guessing God,* pp. 76, 77

7. Why do you think trials and hardship make some people mean and bitter but make others more compassionate?

APPLY

8. Can you think of a time when you felt compassion for another person and knew that what you were feeling was beyond mere human emotions? What happened?

9. Have trials caused you to become more bitter and angry? Take a risk and be transparent. Look at the list of statements below and choose which one best reflects how you can take a step toward becoming a more compassionate person:

- ❏ I need to forgive.
- ❏ I need to release my bitterness.
- ❏ I need to take myself and life less seriously.
- ❏ I need to learn patience.
- ❏ I need to talk about what happened.
- ❏ I need to ________________ (provide your own statement).

The Main Idea

In his book *I and Thou*, philosopher Martin Buber says there are essentially two kinds of relationships in the world.

"I and Thou" relationships—person to person, and "I and It" relationships—person to object.[3]

Having Jesus' heart for people keeps us from turning people in our lives into *it* people. You know what I mean by *it* people. When we treat the bank teller no differently than we would an ATM machine, we have turned him into an it. When the cashier who takes our order at a drive-thru doesn't even have a face, we've turned her into an it. Sometimes we even live in the same house with *it* people.

Jesus never met an *it* person. Jesus noticed everyone. He had an I-Thou relationship with everyone he met. Every interaction he had with another person meant something to Jesus. He didn't eat a meal and then two minutes later forget the name of the person who served him. That's what having Jesus' *splanchna* does to us. It sensitizes us to people and their needs.

—*Second Guessing God*, pp. 79, 80

10. When life doesn't turn out the way we like, we often ask why. I believe God would like us to begin to train ourselves to ask who. To whom does God want you to reach out with the wisdom and experience this trial has brought into your life?

- Is there an "it" person God wants you to change into a "thou" person?

Together, read this final challenge from the book:

> Frederick Buechner once said, "Compassion is the sometimes fatal capacity for feeling what it's like to live inside somebody else's skin. It is the knowledge that there can never really be any peace and joy for me until there is peace and joy finally for you too."[4]

11. If the pool of Bethesda existed today, what burden would you take to the water's edge? End your group time by praying for those burdens and asking God to help you understand what it's like to live inside each other's skin.

Before the next meeting:

- Read chapters 5 and 8 in *Second Guessing God.*
- Underline anything that you learn for the first time or are inspired by or have a question about.

Leader Follow-up
"Jesus, give me your heart for people." Encourage your group to begin praying that prayer this week. Encourage them to pray for the compassion of Jesus to supernaturally fill their hearts.

NOTES

[1]With permission from the author, Elisabeth Kubler-Ross.

[2]Thornton Wilder, edited by A. Tappan Wilder, *The Collected Short Plays of Thornton Wilder* (New York: Theater Communications Group, 1998), vol. 2, 74–75.

[3]Martin Buber, translated by Ronald Gregor Smith, *I and Thou* (New York: Charles Scribner's Sons, 1958), 3.

[4]Frederick Buechner, *Wishful Thinking: A Seeker's ABC* (New York: HarperSanFrancisco, 1993), 18.

SESSION FOUR

Doubt

It is said that in some countries trees will grow, but will bear no fruit, because there is no winter there.[1]

—*John Bunyan*

Leader Preparation

- ❑ As a child were you allowed to question your parents' ideas and rules? How do you think this affected your outlook on God?
- ❑ Read *Second Guessing God* chapters 5 and 8 and Matthew 28:16-20.
- ❑ Read this lesson beforehand, jotting down your observations and questions as they arise.

CONNECT

1. If you were forced to choose, which would you pick and why?

❑ Getting lost in the middle of a desert

❑ Being abandoned in the middle of the ocean

There have been numerous times in my spiritual walk when my soul felt like it was in a lush oasis of God's presence. There have been other times I've been so full of doubts I thought I had wandered off into a spiritual desert and wouldn't be found until days later, facedown in the sand, disoriented, and on the verge of spiritual death. During those times I've felt abandoned, confused, angry, and worst of all—without hope.

I think the word *desert* is a perfect description of a Christian's experience of God's absence. When *desert* is used in the New Testament, it is a translation of the Greek word *erêmos,* which means "solitary" or "abandoned." This is exactly how I feel when I am experiencing intense doubt. I feel abandoned by God, utterly alone. I feel spiritually lethargic, like I'm lying face down in the sand, dehydrated. During these times of doubt, I have no passion left for participating in church, reading the Bible, prayer, or anything related to God. All I feel is emptiness, as if a large presence just left a room.

The Big Picture

One of the most well-known passages in the Bible is Matthew 28:18-20, referred to by many as the Great Commission because it outlines Jesus' final marching orders for his followers. Over the years I've heard more sermons, read more books, listened to more tapes, and had more discussions around that passage than any other in the Bible. That passage was one of the initial reasons I decided to become a pastor. Churches, mission organizations, colleges, and other ministries around the world point to that passage as the basis for their existence: to help every person on the planet become a follower of Jesus. It's undeniable that Matthew 28:18-20 has become the international rallying cry for Christians everywhere.

—*Second Guessing God*, p. 85, 86

Yet the Bible attests that sometimes our greatest spiritual transformations occur in the desert. For the children of Israel, their forty-year wandering in the desert changed them as a people. Fasting forty days and nights in the desert at the beginning of his ministry marked Jesus. Galatians 1:17 tell us that after the apostle Paul was first converted, he immediately went to Arabia. We're not told how long he was there or what he did, but we do know that he came back a changed person. Spending time in a *spiritual* desert can foster some of our greatest moments of spiritual growth.

2. Take a moment and sketch a quick timeline of your life from birth up to today. Write down major periods of your life like early childhood, teen years, young adulthood, and others. During which period did you feel closest to God? farthest away from God? Why?

STUDY

Read Matthew 28:18-20.

3. As a group, try to boil down Matthew 28:18-20 into a one-sentence mission statement. How effectively is the church or ministry you are a part of fulfilling that mission?

4. Reread the Great Commission, but do so starting at verse 16.

- ❑ Who doubted?
- ❑ What did they doubt?
- ❑ How does reading the two verses preceding that passage affect your understanding of the Great Commission?
- ❑ Does this change the wording of the mission statement your church has created?

5. What are some questions or issues that have caused you to doubt? Are you troubled more by "head" questions (intellectual issues) or "heart" questions (people and fairness issues)?

6. What impact do you think Christians would make in the world if they attempted to fulfill the Great Commission without ever struggling with doubt? Would they be more effective or less? Why?

The Inside Story

For years I skimmed over those preceding verses (vv. 16, 17). Then one day last year I was studying this passage again while preparing for a sermon, and I was struck by the words "some doubted" as if reading them for the first time.

There is great irony in the way those two verses precede Jesus' Great Commission. Jesus' disciples had just spent three years watching him perform awe-inspiring miracles, not to mention his last and greatest miracle of all—rising from the dead. After that experience, the last people on earth one would ever suspect of doubting are these eleven disciples. Aside from this, it's ironic that Matthew chose to include "some doubted" at all. Couldn't he have left those words out? I'm sure he was tempted to gloss over this seemingly minor incident, but he didn't. Why? I believe he deliberately penned these words because he wanted to communicate a very important truth to all future Christians: struggling with doubt is a natural part of being a follower of Jesus.

—*Second Guessing God*, p. 87

The Main Idea

At the heart of a life filled with unanswered questions lies the very nature of Christianity. Our faith is about a relationship with Jesus, not an adherence to a set of intellectual ideas we can memorize and master. Doubt reminds us of this. In Matthew 28:16-20, the disciples could walk away from that mountain and continue to follow Jesus with all their doubts because they were following *him*—a real, living, breathing person—not a book. Jesus and his disciples were in relationship with each other, and that relationship took precedence over the disciples' need to have all their questions answered.

—*Second Guessing God*, p. 95

7. Why do you think some churches and church leaders discourage their members from openly discussing tough questions regarding their faith?

- THEY FEEL VULNERABLE - PEOPLE MAY FEEL OTHERS KNOW TOO MUCH!

APPLY

8. Have you ever gone from being on top of the spiritual world into "oh-my-life-is-horrible-and-there-is-no-God" mode? Why do you think this happens?

9. Can you think of some ways experiencing doubt has actually helped your faith grow? Give specific examples.

10. Imagine you are standing alongside the disciples at the top of the mountain, as mentioned in Matthew 28:18-20. Jesus knows every doubt you have hidden in your heart. What kind of expression does he have on his face as he looks you in the eyes?

Together, read this final challenge from the book:

Jesus saw the practical benefits of allowing our doubts to find some fresh air. Describing her own spiritual journey, Madeleine L'Engle wrote, "I had yet to learn the *faithfulness* of doubt. This is often assumed by the judgmental to be faith*less*ness, but it is not; it is a prerequisite for a living faith."[2] I think Jesus felt the same way.

11. Close your group study by praying for one another. Thank God for allowing doubt and using it to grow your faith.

Before the next meeting:

- Read chapter 9 in *Second Guessing God.*
- Underline anything that you learn for the first time or are inspired by or have a question about.

Leader Follow-up
Make sure you take time to affirm the members of your group who openly shared their doubts. One of the most important things you can do to help your group grow closer to Jesus and each other is to foster a culture of honesty and acceptance.

NOTES

[1]John Bunyan, *Advice to Sufferers* (Swengel: Reiner Publications, 1968), 9.

[2]Madeleine L'Engle, *Walking on Water: Reflections on Faith and Art* (Colorado Springs: Waterbrook Press, 2004), 135.

SESSION FIVE

Church

Leader Preparation

- ❏ Do you have a close Christian friend with whom you can share anything? How has having that person (or not having such a person) changed your spiritual walk? Take a moment and reflect on the depth of your Christian friendships.
- ❏ Read *Second Guessing God* chapter 9 and 1 Corinthians 12:12-26.
- ❏ Read this lesson beforehand, jotting down your observations and questions as they arise.

The early Christians were not people of standing, but they had a secret power among them, and the secret power resulted from the way in which they were members of one another.[1]

—*Elton Trueblood*

CONNECT

1. What is the strangest church you've ever visited? What made it so different?

A few years ago another pastor and I traveled to Orlando to attend a church conference. One afternoon we had a break, so we decided to take a "field trip" to Disney World and experience the park from a leadership perspective, asking ourselves what makes the park "the happiest place on earth" as Disney parks are known. We interviewed anyone who would talk to us and learned unforgettable lessons. The signage was amazing. The attention to detail was spectacular. Everything was done to create "just the perfect moment" for people all over the world. The thing that stuck with me the most was what happened in the parking lot as we arrived. Boarding the tram, I noticed a car in the distance with all four doors open wide and security guards rummaging through it. I leaned over to the tram driver and said, "Terrorists?"

"No, tourists," he replied. "They left their car running, doors wide open, and ran for the entrance."

I said, "That has to be the most hysterical thing I've ever heard. Has it ever happened before?"

He looked at me over his shoulder and said, "About five or six times a day!"

Over the years I've been to Disney World a few times, and I've been in a few groups committed to living out Jesus' message. I have to say that my initial excitement for Disney blew away my initial interest in being a part of my groups. When we first met in homes or at the church, it was more than a little awkward. It took time to get to know one another and to trust each other. We had to navigate through the initial stages of personality conflicts and power struggles. We had to say good-bye to a few people who found out they really weren't interested in doing life Jesus' way. Yet over time, as we stuck with it, a simple mystery began to unfold: Jesus showed up.

On occasion we'd sense his presence and then it would be gone. Over time, the deeper we shared, the harder we prayed, and the more we encouraged each other to obey, the more he seemed to leave his footprints in the carpet of the room. Those times together created a thirst unlike anything I had ever experienced. On those days I had to make sure I turned my car off and shut my car doors; I was that excited about being together with my friends. The only difference between those times and the few times I walked onto Main Street, U.S.A., in Orlando was that my experience with my Christian friends was real. Yours will be too, if you take a risk and start small.

The Big Picture

Tucked in the middle of a discussion about the nature of the church, the apostle Paul compared the church to a human body: "If one part suffers, every part suffers with it; if one part is honored, every part rejoices with it" (1 Corinthians 12:26). Paul clearly points out that when we as followers of Jesus become spiritually intimate with one another, it is as if our souls grow together and we begin to share spiritual nerve endings. If something happens to you, I can't help but be affected by it. We are connected soul to soul. In the same way a twisted ankle affects every other part of a human body, the hurt a church member feels touches everyone else in that community. In a healthy-functioning community of Jesus followers, people are deeply connected to one another, and when something happens, good or bad, the instinctive response is to rally around one another. —*Second Guessing God*, pp. 167, 168

2. Have you ever been a part of a church group or class where Jesus' presence was so real that it seemed as if he "left his footprints" on the carpet? What happened in the group to facilitate this?

STUDY

Read 1 Corinthians 12:12-26.

3. What problem was occurring in the Corinthian church that Paul addresses in 1 Corinthians 12?

- If someone had a more publicly noticed gift like teaching or prophecy, how would they have heard Paul's words?
- How would someone with a less publicly noticed gift have heard his words?

4. Read 1 Corinthians 12:26 again. Can you think of a time when you suffered and another Christian stood by you so passionately it was as if he or she actually suffered with you?

5. Can you think of a time when you really wanted to reach out to a Christian friend for encouragement but chose not to? What stopped you? Are you holding back right now?

6. When you encounter a problem, do you tend to go inward (become quiet and not share) or outward (reach out to others)? Is this good or bad?

The Inside Story

Most Christians don't view the church as a place to go when tough times hit. Or perhaps I should say that most Christians who have been followers of Jesus for more than a few years *used* to view the church as a place to go for support when tough times hit. In my experience most Christians become so disappointed with the lack of response to their needs by the church that they stop reaching out. They signed up for Christianity expecting to find authentic, caring relationships, but over time they have had to settle for superficial handshakes and "thinking about you" cards.

—*Second Guessing God*, pp. 164, 165

7. Do you think it is easier to live in community with others if you are an extrovert (i.e., people person)? Why or why not?

8. Many Christians get hurt because their pastor does not reach out to them when they go through tough times. According to 1 Corinthians 12, church members are to care for each other. How do you think we strayed so far from the biblical model of the way church is supposed to operate?

APPLY

9. In the New Testament it is common to find a command that includes the phrase "one another." Look up the following verses and talk about how your group would change if you actually began obeying these commands as a group:

- Romans 12:10
- Galatians 6:1, 2
- Ephesians 4:32
- 1 Thessalonians 5:11
- James 5:16

The Main Idea

My grandmother was born in 1923 and grew up during the Great Depression. She told me that during that difficult time, people wandered door to door with their children, asking for food scraps. People quickly found out that my grandmother's parents were generous people. Anyone who came to the door received food if there was any to give. After a while so many people were coming to their house that they wondered how news of their generosity had spread. One day my great-grandfather inquired, and he was told, "Because of the *X*." On the side of the house, someone had scratched a large *X* that signaled to people walking by that this house was a place you could get your needs met. My advice to you is the same: find some people in your church and mark each other with an *X*. Look each other in the eye and say, "We're going to live in community with one another. We don't know exactly what that looks like right now, but we're making a commitment today to live as followers of Jesus *together* and find out."

—*Second Guessing God*, pp. 172, 173

10. The key to allowing real Christian community to blossom is a radical commitment to being authentic. Go around your group and have each person finish the following statement:

My biggest fear that keeps me from letting my guard down in this group is: ____

Together, read this final challenge from the book:
C. S. Lewis once said in his masterful book *The Four Loves*:

> Love anything, and your heart will certainly be wrung and possibly be broken. If you want to make sure of keeping it intact, you must give your heart to no one, not even to an animal. Wrap it carefully round with hobbies and little luxuries; avoid all entanglements; lock it up safe in the casket or coffin of your selfishness. But in that casket—safe, dark, motionless, airless—it will change. It will not be broken; it will become unbreakable, impenetrable, irredeemable.[2]

Don't let this happen to you. Make the decision right now that you're going to step out and risk living in Christian community.

11. End your time together by praying for one another, specifically for the fears expressed in response to question 10.

Leader Follow-up
Continue to remind the members of your group to reach out to each other during the week for support and encouragement. Challenge them to call each other first before turning to the pastor at your church.

Before the next meeting:
- Read chapter 10 in *Second Guessing God.*
- Underline anything that you learn for the first time or are inspired by or have a question about.

NOTES

[1]Elton Trueblood, *The Yoke of Christ* (Waco: Word Books, 1975), 25–26.

[2]C. S. Lewis, *The Four Loves* (New York: Harcourt, 1988), 121.

Ministry

The extreme greatness of Christianity lies in the fact that it does not seek a supernatural remedy for suffering, but a supernatural use for it.[1]

—*Simone Weil*

Leader Preparation

- ❑ Read Simone Weil's quote above. Would you agree with her statement? Do you feel like you have found a supernatural use for the pain God has allowed you to experience in life?
- ❑ Read *Second Guessing God* chapter 10 and Matthew 16:21-28.
- ❑ Read this lesson beforehand, jotting down your observations and questions as they arise.

CONNECT

1. When you went to the doctor's office as a child and it came time to get a shot, how did you react? Choose one of the responses below and give an example:

- I'm tough—I stared at the needle while it happened.
- I climbed up my parent's leg and screamed like a baby.
- I tried to negotiate with the doctor.
- I turned away and stared at the wall.
- I went down swinging.
- I knew it was coming, so I had time to mentally prepare.

In John Bunyan's classic allegory of the Christian life, *The Pilgrim's Progress,* the central character Christian flees the City of Destruction and seeks eternal life. During his long pilgrimage he walks on the narrow path of the Hill of Difficulty, down through the Valley of Humiliation, passes through the Valley of the Shadow of Death, and eventually reaches the Celestial City. Along the way he meets the characters Mr. Worldly Wiseman, Hopeful, and Faithful. At one point on his journey, Christian narrowly escapes the Doubting Castle, which is guarded by the Giant Despair. Thinking that those following behind him might fall into the giant's lethal grip, he decides to make a sign to warn future sojourners about the giant. The sign he erected read:

> Over this stile is the way to *Doubting Castle;* which is kept by Giant *Despair,* who despiseth the King of the *Celestial Country,* and seeks to destroy his holy pilgrims.

Then Bunyan adds:

> Many, therefore, that followed after, read what was written, and escaped the danger.[2]

I must not have been paying attention while I was pastoring in Ohio, because I blew right past that sign. During that time my soul was in the grip of the giant. I was miserable beyond description. I was angry, bitter, depressed. I slept too much, ate too much, and withdrew from people. I stopped smiling. This was one pilgrim the giant had no problem overpowering. Then something happened: the more I served people, the more wiggle room I noticed in the giant's grip. Over time, while throwing myself into the lives of other people, serving them, and loving them, each act of love and service brought me a little closer to home.

Do you find yourself in the lethal grasp of despair right now? God has provided a second way for you to hold on during life's difficult moments. In addition to living in authentic Christian community, serve others. As you serve others in the midst of your pain—orienting your entire mind, heart, and soul around serving others in Jesus' name—the giant's grip on your soul will loosen.

2. After you became a believer and encountered your first real period of hardship, were you surprised? Did you feel like you had ample explanation of how hard the Christian life might be, or did you feel like someone pulled a "bait and switch"?

The Big Picture

The word Jesus uses for "life" in Matthew 16:25 is the Greek word *psyche,* which is the Greek word for "soul." The soul, according to Jesus, has its own way of making itself better, but it also has its own way of becoming toxic. Ultimately, the health of the soul is dependent upon the way we orient our lives. We become spiritually sick when, like incessantly scratching our poison ivy, we become obsessed with our own pain. NICOLE

According to Jesus, one of the ways soul wounds heal is by leaving them alone and focusing the energy we're tempted to expend on them outside ourselves instead. I do not want to imply that seeking counseling, acquiring medical treatment, setting clear personal boundaries, or taking care of ourselves emotionally and physically are wrong. I believe these activities can be an important part of "losing our lives." Learning to give up our demand for everyone else to make us happy and taking responsibility for our own lives is extremely important. But even these positive activities can be taken to the extreme if we're not careful.

That's why balancing self-care with serving is so important: it takes the focus off me in a natural way. It breaks me out of any possibility of self-obsession, no matter how well intended.

—*Second Guessing God,* pp. 187, 188

STUDY

Read Matthew 16:21-28.

3. In verse 23 Jesus goes ballistic on Peter. What was at stake for Jesus to react so strongly? Satan was trying to make Jesus change his mind.

4. Verse 25 is a perfect example of Jesus' use of paradox—a seemingly contradictory statement that is nonetheless true. What did Jesus mean by this statement? How would Peter have understood his words? Give up your life for Christ

example of shepard

5. One of the scariest things about going through dark periods in our lives is the way proven spiritual practices like prayer and Bible study seem to lose their potency. Do you think that during these times we're meant to stop praying and reading our Bibles and do something else to connect with God? Why? Why not?

The Inside Story

I know this will sound sacrilegious, but the most important advice I can give you, if you are having trouble hanging on, is this: if you can't pray, stop trying to pray. Gather all your devotional books and prayer journals and throw them into a box. Run away from churches advertising sermons on prayer and all of the other neat, American, utilitarian approaches to connecting to God. Give yourself permission to connect with God in another fashion. If it lasts a week, so be it. If it lasts three months, so be it. Enter into a season of serving and listening and be perfectly content with that. As Oswald Chambers said in his spiritual classic *My Utmost for His Highest*, "Are you in the dark just now in your circumstances, or in your life with God? Then remain quiet. If you open your mouth in the dark, you will talk in the wrong mood: darkness is the time to listen."[4]

—*Second Guessing God*, p. 195

6. Doesn't it seem counterintuitive to think that we get better when we serve others? Can you think of some examples when this occurred in your own life? Why do you think this happens?

7. Can you think of a time when you did the exact opposite of what Jesus instructed and oriented everything you did to "find your life"? Did it work? What did you end up "losing" in the end?

APPLY

8. Reflect on the week preceding your group's meeting and write down in each category all activities where you either sought to "find your life" or "lose your life." Do you think the way you allocated your time and energy affected your sense of joy and fulfillment? What changes will you make this week to bring these two columns into balance?

Finding Life	Losing Life
______________	______________
______________	______________
______________	______________
______________	______________
______________	______________
______________	______________

9. Think of someone that you are going to go out of your way and serve this week. Place his or her name in the box below. Share with the group why you picked this person and how you're going to serve him or her.

Together, read this final challenge from the book:

> One second-century Christian document called *The Didache*, which means "The Teaching," began its instruction to new Christians this way: "There are two Ways: a Way of Life and a Way of Death, and the difference between these two Ways is great."[6] Are you hurting? Do you feel like you can't break out of the giant's grip? Choose the path that leads to life. Ignore what your intuition tells you and break outside yourself in order to serve others in spite of your pain. Heal your wounds by focusing your energy elsewhere. Trust Jesus' instruction that as we focus on others we find our souls again.

The Main Idea

The question we need to ask ourselves when God allows us to go through hard times is not why but who? In the mind of God, pain always has two intended recipients: us and someone else. If we choose not to take what we've experienced and find some way of using it to help other people, we miss a large part of why God allowed us to suffer in the first place.

In his book *The Gospel of Suffering*, philosopher Søren Kierkegaard asked:

> When indeed does the temporal suffering oppress a man most terribly? Is it not when it seems to him that it has no significance, that it neither secures nor gains anything for him? Is it not when the suffering, as the impatient man expresses it, is without meaning or purpose?[5]

Absolutely. Suffering is pointless when it is without meaning, and suffering is without meaning, ultimately, when what we've suffered isn't put to some greater use.

—*Second Guessing God*, p. 196

10. Close your time together by praying for each other. Make sure you pray for each other's efforts to reach out and serve others in Jesus' name this week.

Before the next meeting:

- Read chapter 11 in *Second Guessing God.*
- Underline anything that you learn for the first time or are inspired by or have a question about.

Leader Follow-up
Since next week's session will be the last session for this study, make sure you encourage your group to finish reading any chapters they have skipped up to this point.

NOTES

[1]Simone Weil, translated by Arthur Wills, *Gravity and Grace* (New York: G. P. Putnam's Sons, 1952), 132.

[2]John Bunyan, *The Pilgrim's Progress* (New York: The Heritage Press, 1942), 137.

[3]Colin Brown, ed., *The New International Dictionary of New Testament Theology* (Grand Rapids: Regency Reference Library, 1986), vol. 3, 676.

[4]Oswald Chambers, *My Utmost for His Highest* (New York: Dodd, Mead & Company, 1935), 45.

[5]Søren Kierkegaard, translated by David F. Swenson and Lillian Marvin Swenson, *The Gospel of Suffering* (Minneapolis: Augsburg, 1948), 126–127.

[6]"The Didache" in *Early Christian Writings* (New York, NY: Viking Penguin, Inc., 1987), 191.

SESSION SEVEN

Heaven

I divested myself of despair and fear when I came here.[1]

—*Jane Kenyon*

Leader Preparation

- ❑ For you, personally, why is Heaven going to be so great? Because of the people you'll see there? Leaving earthly problems behind? Being with Jesus? What makes you long for Heaven?
- ❑ Read *Second Guessing God* chapter 11 and Revelation 21:1-5.
- ❑ Read this lesson beforehand, jotting down your observations and questions as they arise.

CONNECT

1. The Bible tells us that we get new bodies when we go to Heaven. What's one thing about your "old body" you're not going to miss?

On July 24, 2000, I told a bald-faced lie. Our family was at Walt Disney World's Epcot Center® for a vacation, and after paying for our tickets we were told by a security guard that we wouldn't be allowed to bring our baby stroller inside. The temperature that day was ninety-nine degrees; our youngest daughter was only eight months old but weighed nearly thirty pounds, and carrying her around all day in the sweltering heat seemed unthinkable. The security officer said that if we went to the main security pavilion we might be able to get a special exemption, so I wheeled her to the office and went inside.

"Sir," a woman told me, "we cannot give you a permit to use your stroller inside the park."

I countered, "I wish you would have told us that before we purchased our nonrefundable tickets. There's no way I can carry her around all day."

Then she asked, "Does she have a special medical condition? If so, I can give you a permit that you can put on her stroller that will allow you to enter each ride and exhibit through the handicapped access."

I paused. Wheels started turning. I was desperate. I was stupid. I was sweaty. I anticipated needing back surgery after the long drive home. I looked outside at my daughters jumping up and down, waiting to go inside, and then I did it: I leaned over and said, "Uh, she's got FBS syndrome."

"Well, why didn't you mention that when you came in?"

"It's rare," I told her. "I don't like drawing attention to it."

She scribbled "FBS syndrome" on a little yellow tag and handed it to me. "Place this on your stroller handle and show it to the operator of each ride and exhibit. They'll let you right in."

I thanked her and walked out the door, knowing full well that I was headed straight toward the pit of Hell. I showed my wife the yellow tag. "What's FBS syndrome?" she asked.

I whispered in her ear, "Fat baby syndrome."

Lisa laughed, "She's not fat!"

"Have you held her lately?" I said.

The rest of the day, despite the protest of my wife, we used the stroller and rode every ride and walked through every exhibit. The only problem was having to use the handicapped access. As the day unfolded, I began to wonder if God wasn't using my lie to teach me a greater lesson.

At first I thought it was funny that we were able to bypass hour-long lines and walk straight to the front of a ride. Then I started to notice the people with whom we were spending time: mentally challenged children in wheelchairs, adults with cerebral palsy, kids on ventilators. I'll never forget the image of one young boy who needed three Epcot workers just to help load his wheelchair onto a ramp. His head gently lay to the side on a headrest, and his arms were strapped to the wheelchair with large black bands. Behind his back sat a large computer that regulated his breathing. His parents and two brothers walked slowly at his side, adjusting his breathing tube as the Epcot employees gently maneuvered his wheelchair onto the ride.

That day marked me. For twelve long hours, ride after ride after ride, I was given a front-row-seat view of the painful lives of the physically broken. For the people at Epcot that day, Heaven will be a day of liberation. There are no ventilators in Heaven, no handicapped access ramps, no beds with rails. No one needs someone else to bathe them, feed them, push their wheelchair, write for them, or hold the phone up to their ear. In 1 Corinthians 15:42, 43, God promises a new beginning for them all. "The body that is sown is perishable, it is raised imperishable; it is sown in dishonor, it is raised in glory; it is sown in weakness, it is raised in power." What an amazing day that will be.

2. What are you looking forward to most about Heaven?

STUDY

Read Revelation 21:1-5.

3. Many of the original readers of Revelation were suffering. How would this depiction be reassuring to them?

4. Verse 3 tells us that "God himself will be with them." Does that excite you? make you fearful? no reaction? Why?

The Main Idea

C. S. Lewis said, "A book on suffering which says nothing of heaven, is leaving out almost the whole of one side of the account. Scripture and tradition habitually put the joys of heaven into the scale against the sufferings of earth, and no solution of the problem of pain which does not do so can be called a Christian one."[2]

The Inside Story

In Heaven family members don't discover the bodies of loved ones who have committed suicide. No one dies in automobile accidents, on operating tables, or from old age. There are no strange food allergies, people shed their mental illnesses like old coats before they go there, and there's never any need to take sleeping pills. Memories of mistakes we made as parents don't haunt us anymore. No one is considered ugly. There's no minimum wage, no wars or terrorists or military budgets, no tsunamis, earthquakes, hurricanes, or tornados. There's no such thing as an addiction, and no need to leave flowers on anyone's grave. Tumors can't ravage our bodies in Heaven, and no one steps across homeless people while getting on the bus.

—*Second Guessing God*, p. 212

5. What do you expect your response to be when you enter God's presence?

- If you knew you wouldn't be zapped, do you think you'd get angry?
- Would it be inauthentic of you *not* to get angry after what you've experienced?

6. Admittedly, there's much less information in the Bible describing what Heaven will be like than we'd prefer. Based on Revelation 21:1-5, what can we realistically know about Heaven?

7. What do you think we'll do in Heaven? Will it matter?

8. Some have commented that the Bible's description of Heaven sounds boring. Do you agree or disagree? Why?

APPLY

9. What has been the biggest "aha" moment you've had throughout this seven-week study?

10. There's an old saying: "Live like you'll die tomorrow. Die knowing you'll live forever." Is that really possible? How would taking that statement literally change the way you live?

Together, read this final challenge from the book:

> Throughout this book we've spent a great deal of time talking about all the possible reasons why God has allowed us to suffer and how we can hang on during those difficult times. One day very soon all of that won't matter any longer. One day, the chemo drips will end, the nights spent wondering where God is leading you next will come to a close, and all of the anxiety you've felt worrying about your son or daughter will evaporate before your very eyes. On that day your need for answers will fade into the background as you notice someone walking toward you on the faint horizon. Shrouded in light, you'll barely be able to make out the silhouette. But as each step brings him closer toward you, you'll begin to feel a sense of certainty, a weightlessness you've never felt before, the brief pain of expectation in your chest. This longing, a feeling you've but touched as it grazed your soul during your time on earth, this presence will be standing right before your very eyes. Jesus will smile, hold out his arms, and suddenly all the pain and suffering you've endured in this life will be lost in his grasp as he utters the words you've been longing to hear: "Welcome home. Welcome home."

11. Close your study by praying for each other. Thank God for what you have learned through your study as a group, and let Jesus know how much you are looking forward to his embrace.

Leader Follow-up
Thank your group members for their time and participation. Let them know how much you've enjoyed their honest questions and thoughtful discussions.

NOTES

[1]Jane Kenyon, "Notes from the Other Side," *Constance: Poems* (St. Paul: Graywolf Press, 1993), 59.

[2]C. S. Lewis, *The Problem of Pain* (New York: HarperCollins, 1996), 148.

Maintaining Spiritual Focus

by Rick Lowry

Small group leadership can be a detail-intensive ministry. Lesson preparation and regular contact with group members are hard enough to squeeze into a busy leader's calendar. Add to these the scheduling of hosts and refreshments, information updates, and attendance at training sessions, and it becomes one of the most demanding ministries in the church.

With all these elements to keep up with, it is easy to lose spiritual focus. Here are some ways that I, as a small group leader, maintain my spiritual focus.

GROWTH ATMOSPHERE. A small group leader can provide a positive atmosphere for spiritual growth. Above all else, my goal as a small group leader is the spiritual success of the individuals God has placed under my spiritual care. I am willing to do whatever it takes for the members to find God's will for their lives and to help them move in an upward direction. As their shepherd, I am coming to God on my knees and saying, "God, please give me insight into each person's life in my group, so I can determine what exactly they need in order to move to the next spiritual level."

BIBLICAL FOUNDATION. Spiritual leadership means making the Bible the foundation of group life. We rightly think of small groups as a tremendous relational opportunity. But as vital as relationship building is in small groups, the Word of God is still the foundation. It should be obvious to any visitor to our group meeting, any random week, that the Bible is essential to us.

PERSONAL HOLINESS. The most important thing I can do to lead my flock spiritually is to be spiritual myself. I cannot lead people to a place I have not been (or maybe even am not willing to go).

My daily prayer is "Lord, how closely am I walking with you?" I have developed ten questions to ask myself on a regular basis to make sure I am knowing God more deeply:

- Holiness: Am I progressively moving away from sin?
- God's Word: Is God's Word food to me, and am I spending time in it?
- Worship: Am I worshiping regularly, both privately and corporately?
- Sharing faith: Am I sharing my faith regularly?
- Stretching faith: Am I stretching my faith regularly, stepping out of my comfort zone to a place where I depend on God?
- Prayer: Am I daily talking and listening to God in prayer?
- Solitude: Have I been alone with God enough to hear his voice clearly?
- Serving: Am I serving with the abilities God has given me?
- Spiritual progress: Am I further along in my relationship with God than I was a year ago?
- Accountability: Have I made myself accountable to another trustworthy brother or sister for my spiritual maintenance and growth?

If I can answer yes to those ten, I can be fairly sure that I am putting myself in a place to know God more deeply with every year that passes. I can be confident that God can use my leadership to implant spiritual growth in my group members.

I have been to groups where people seem afraid to talk about spiritual things. Most people won't automatically gravitate toward spiritual concerns in a group discussion. They look to the leader to open the spiritual door and invite them in.

INTIMATE KNOWLEDGE. A spiritual leader knows his or her group members well. This takes time, building trust and expressing interest.

This knowledge begins with the little things. Do I have the birthdays of the people in my group on my calendar? Can I name their children? Do I know their struggles? Do I know how they best connect? Is she a studier? Is he a person for whom relationships are important? Which ones are oriented more toward feeling or thinking?

Jesus modeled a depth of care as he who lays down his "life for the sheep." When was the last time I made a sacrifice to see my group members grow in Christ—a sacrifice of time perhaps, doing a little extra preparation to give this week's lesson a creative edge? Or a sacrifice of energy to get them involved in a service project. A good leader knows the group members and chooses activities based on their spiritual needs.

VALLEY WALKING. A good leader walks with group members in their spiritual valleys. Romans 12:15 encourages us to "Rejoice with those who rejoice; mourn with those who mourn." That means we have taken the time to enter into the joys and pains of the life of another person, a vulnerable and risky business.

Members experiencing a spiritual valley will sometimes shy away from the group with whom they previously enjoyed fellowship. A wise group leader will go to them, offer assurance, and even help heal relationships that may be strained.

PRAYER AND DEPENDENCE. I will never experience any spiritual success if I attempt to lead my small group by my own power and wisdom. I must depend on God. I must pray daily and fervently for God to do his work among my group members. As I lead, I keep my eyes on Jesus. He went to the trouble of purchasing his people with his own blood. He will not refuse wisdom to those of us he has called to aid in the spiritual formation of his redeemed.

FREE Small Group Resources

With the purchase of this book, you are entitled to a free 1-month membership at www.SmallGroups.com where you can get even more small group resources like this article. To claim your FREE membership:

- Go to: www.SmallGroups.com/freemembership
- Continue through "checkout" process
- Select payment method "check/money order." However, no payment is due if you use the coupon code: stdsg06
- Then click "Redeem" and "Confirm Order" for your free membership.